NOV 16

SCIENCE AT WORK

MASS

AT

WORK

LAUREN KUKLA

Consulting Editor, Diane Craig, M.A./Reading Specialist

Sandcastle

An Imprint of Abdo Publishing
abdopublishing.com

abdopublishing.com

Published by Abdo Publishing, a division of ABDO, PO Box 398166, Minneapolis, Minnesota 55439. Copyright © 2017 by Abdo Consulting Group, Inc. International copyrights reserved in all countries. No part of this book may be reproduced in any form without written permission from the publisher. SandCastle™ is a trademark and logo of Abdo Publishing.

Printed in the United States of America, North Mankato, Minnesota

062016
092016

Design: Mighty Media, Inc.
Content Developer: Nancy Tuminelly
Production: Mighty Media, Inc.
Editor: Liz Salzmann
Photo Credits: NASA, Shutterstock

Library of Congress Cataloging-in-Publication Data

Names: Kukla, Lauren, author.
Title: Mass at work / Lauren Kukla ; consulting editor, Diane Craig, M.A./reading specialist.
Description: Minneapolis, Minnesota : Abdo Publishing, [2017] | Series: Science at work
Identifiers: LCCN 2016000312 (print) | LCCN 2016005192 (ebook) | ISBN 9781680781434 (print) | ISBN 9781680775877 (ebook)
Subjects: LCSH: Mass (Physics)--Juvenile literature. | Gravity--Juvenile literature.
Classification: LCC QC106 .K85 2017 (print) | LCC QC106 (ebook) | DDC 531.14--dc23
LC record available at http://lccn.loc.gov/2016000312

SandCastle™ Level: Fluent

SandCastle™ books are created by a team of professional educators, reading specialists, and content developers around five essential components—phonemic awareness, phonics, vocabulary, text comprehension, and fluency—to assist young readers as they develop reading skills and strategies and increase their general knowledge. All books are written, reviewed, and leveled for guided reading, early reading intervention, and Accelerated Reader™ programs for use in shared, guided, and independent reading and writing activities to support a balanced approach to literacy instruction. The SandCastle™ series has four levels that correspond to early literacy development. The levels are provided to help teachers and parents select appropriate books for young readers.

EMERGING · BEGINNING · TRANSITIONAL · FLUENT

CONTENTS

ABOUT MASS

Have you ever watched a train slow to a stop? Or hit a baseball?

This is mass
at work!

Mass measures how much **matter** an object has. A cow has a lot of mass.

A feather has less mass. Mass is
the same everywhere.

What is the difference between mass and weight?

Weight measures the pull of **gravity** on an object.

The United States measures
weight in pounds.

Most other
countries measure
in kilograms.

Tyson uses a scale.
He weighs himself.

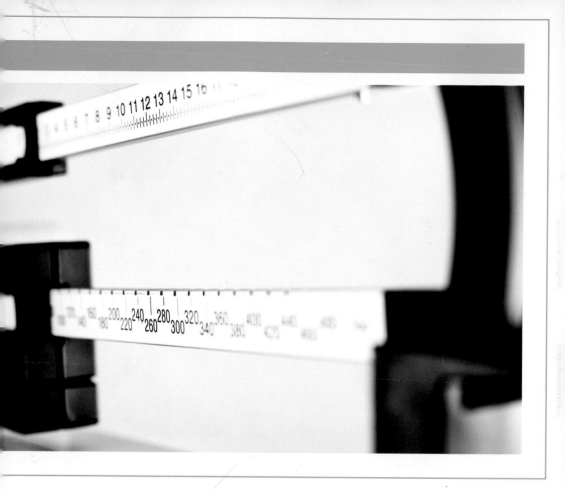

He weighs 50 pounds.
That is 23 kilograms.

Weight changes away from Earth.
The moon has less **gravity**.

An **astronaut** weighs less on the moon.
The astronaut's mass stays the same.

Mass is not the same as size. Nate's
balloon is big. But it has little mass.

Gia's rocks are smaller.
But they have more mass.

Many scientists have studied mass.
Isaac Newton studied **physics**.

He looked at how mass changes
motion.

Objects with more mass are harder to stop. A bus has a lot of mass.

A bike has less mass. The bike can stop more easily.

THINK ABOUT IT

Look around you! Where else is mass at work? How do you use it?

GLOSSARY

astronaut – a person who is trained to travel in space.

gravity – a force that pulls things toward Earth and other planets.

matter – anything that has weight and takes up space.

physics – the science that studies matter and energy.